THE WORD FOR WHEN

THE WORD FOR WHEN

poems by
Denise Rogers

University of Louisiana at Lafayette Press
2025

http://ulpress.org
University of Louisiana at Lafayette Press
P.O. Box 43558
Lafayette, LA 70504-3558

Library of Congress Cataloging-in-Publication Data

Names: Rogers, Denise, 1957- author.
Title: The word for when / Denise Rogers.
Other titles: Word for when (Compilation)
Description: Lafayette, LA : University of Louisiana at Lafayette Press, 2025.
Identifiers: LCCN 2024054318 | ISBN 9781959569206 (paperback)
Subjects: LCGFT: Poetry.
Classification: LCC PS3618.O45766 W67 2025 | DDC 811/.6--dc23/eng/20241120
LC record available at https://lccn.loc.gov/2024054318

cover image: *Kamo Village on Sado Island* (*Sado Kamoson*), from the series *Souvenirs of Travel II* (*Tabi miyage dai nishû*) by Kawase Hasui

Acknowledgments

These poems, sometimes in other versions, were published in the following journals. I thank all of the editors who selected my work to appear in their publications.

"An Idea of North," "Louisiana Snowfall," "From a City Girl to Han Shan, Somewhere on Cold Mountain," *Journal of College Writing* 13 (2017): 43–51.

"The Emperor's Dreams," *MockingHeart Review* 2, no. 1 (2017), https://mockingheartreview.com/archives/volume-2-issue-1/.

"The Lovers," "A Loss," and "Tu Fu Dreams of Fishing with Mrs. Tu," *word-river literary review* (2011): 20, 83, 101.

"Regarding Dr. Gachet," in *The Southern Poetry Anthology: Vol. 4: Louisiana,* ed. William Wright (Huntsville: Texas Review Press, 2011), 198.

"Francis and the Birds," *The Ekphrastic Review*, October 4, 2020, https://www.ekphrastic.net/.

"Triptych (The Way to Read a Triptych)," *Louisiana Review* (Spr./Sum. 2009): 14.

"The Word for When," *Sliver of Stone*, no. 3 (Sept. 2011), https://sliverofstonemagazine.com/denise-rogers/.

CONTENTS

Part I: Now

Part II: Then

Part III: When

Part I

Now

Hippopotamus Alone Before a Swatch Kiosk in Tblisi

*Based on "Zoo Animals Escape Amid Heavy Flooding
in Tblisi." Photograph by Beso Gulashvili / Reuters.*

How did I find myself here
knee-high in water
looking at swatches of watches?
All around me people stare.

A few of the children say not to
get too near.
They have heard
from their programs that I can be fierce.
Dear children, it's when I need to be,
or when I'm like you,
afraid and disconcerted.

So much confusion around me
in Tblisi today
for a hippopotamus amidst
such flooding.

This morning when the skies burst
for another day, it seemed
the world had finally
become familiar. I could move
in it the way I dreamt of
when I was young and heard the stories
from my grandmother.

But it's not the same, not really,
with the heaps of trash in the street.
Ask the poor bear cub

holding onto a concrete block
while all around him float green
soda bottles.

A man saves a penguin
streaked with mud. A hippo
wades out among flooded cars.
Who knows what to do?
Even swans can't make the lakes
in the streets lovely
when the bear cub's mother lies prone
and wasted on an old door
next to her.

So I just stand here, hoping to see
a face I know with a lure
and direction.
I know they are not gods,
or family.
I will need to make a decision
soon
whether they are friends
or still
my enemy.

**From a City Girl to Hanshan,
Somewhere on Cold Mountain**

I walk among mist-saturated trees
that are luminous. At the edge
of the field I stop to watch egrets
float across the field: white banners
signaling a truce with summer.

The only mountains here, old friend,
are bales of hay clouds drifting above.
Their casual pace is a meditation,
mirroring my own efforts at peace.

O, Hanshan, how did you leave
the city behind? Did you miss it
when you fled to your Mountain?

Or did you bring a piece
of it with you, a lump
on your back, lugged
along in a sack?

It wasn't all peace for you poets,
back then, like it isn't
for us today. You sang
the old songs you learned
at court in backwater bars.
We sing the ones we know
in taverns and dancehalls.

Last night in the rain,
I was missing home,
but then I heard the hum

of those little tunes
you once sang to an audience
of crickets visiting
your tiny room.

I'm humming along tonight
to a calico cat
and three dozen katydids.
I sit at my own dark desk,
and write, a rucksack
of my home earth
keeping company
on the floor beside me.

Some Front Yards in Lonedell

The hollowed-out cars
in the yards
along 47
are much like headstones
or poems,
depending on the angle: abandoned
but not left. Loved
but not lost.

Dashboards and chassis
up on blocks or
underneath a greying tarp,
there are parts
worth salvaging,
somebody knows,
or why keep them?

Each one's an epitaph
to a greater whole.

Each one's a dream
of what once was,
and more importantly,
like their owners,
what might
yet be.

Louisiana Snowfall

It's usually gone
by eight if it comes
at six, its tiny feet
like fog.

Snow's a sigh here,
an effervescence
sprinkled stingily
on lanes and byways.

Its momentary luster,
sheen of eau-de-vie
kisses the bristles
of your dark brow.

I forgive it for being
ethereal and sweet,
a wisp of frost
to hang onto.

This is a wet,
nostalgic place,
so snow leaves
aches.

They're like those
cemetery angels
that can't help but wrench
your heart a little
out of place.

This snow, *ma chère*,
is made of jots
of joie de vivre.

It's like the chicory
that wakens coffee:
teaspoonfuls
of sorrow
in the midst
of our affairs.

Passing the Old Place on 47

By now, it would have changed
in all the ways
our childhood places do, anyhow:

front yard twenty feet shorter,
apple tree much smaller,
the white porch now green.

And I'm sure, if it still stood,
the antlers of the buck
my grandpa shot
would no longer hang
above the garage door.

Inside, the rooms would be
empty of violets
and the statues of saints
I'd read about in her *Lives*.

There might still be the yard,
which could be mowed
in an hour and a half,
if three kids had the job.
And the tree in the back,
might have stood twenty
more years, though it never
really was worth climbing,
its apples wormy to eat,
green and hard.

In that little house, my parents
tried to hush my fears

without success.
Winter afternoons
were spent close to the wood stove
if you wouldn't brave the cold
but could stand Grandpa's cigarettes.

Memories will have to do, I guess,
now it's all gone, the house, the garden.
the pump house, the porch,
the trees dredged up
and carted away or buried
beneath the gravel
of the county shed.

A marmoreal calm settles on me,
as the house and its occupants
turn to stone in my reverence.

The old place was no monument,
but its rusted gate led to byways
less mortal than the asphalt ones
I now travel on.

Kingfisher Among Pinks and Irises

After a woodcut by Hiroshige.

Kingfisher darts among ayame irises—
rare blooms among the wetlands of Japan.

The pinks we find among their fronds
are the exact color of your palms.

The bud of the iris is slow to open,
as I know from my garden at home.

My irises may open tomorrow.
If you are there, I won't watch this alone.

Oh, my heart, I want to peel back
the flower's fragile purple folds.

I long to learn what lies
at the tender, fragrant center.

Cherry Blossoms, Tokyo, Spring 2012

> *For Mark*

> *Hanami parties: Expeditions to view*
> *the cherry blossoms,*
> *often under moonlight.*
> *Kami: Shinto nature gods/spirits.*

Hanami parties
are cancelled
this year. The mayor
asks we practice
some restraint.

There is a time
for grief, I know,
but must we
abide amidst it
always?

Cherry blossoms
go on and on,
still competing
with spring clouds
lowering in the sky.

Try to ignore
opened buds
hanging above.
They just keep flowering
white and pink
on a backdrop of blue.

What shall we do
in times like these,
we want to ask.
The Ancients
would have drunk

a toast
to all those gods
at whom
we shake
our fists.

Modern couples
accept their fate,
and ignore the kami
wandering the avenues
at their feet.

Your lives are short!
the pink and white proclaim.
*We will not halt
our yearly show
to mourn.*

We're kissed by grief,
but grief's still life.
Watch how we handle loss,
the cherry blossoms say,
*our petals tears
we gift away.*

Fireflies

Our fathers instructed our fickleness.
       Sunday's patriarch ignored
       his Saturday confederates.

But pickle jar prisons and cricket cages
       were occupations they still recognized.

And when we would bundle our offerings
       of stems and grass,
       leaves and dirt
           (nothing any firefly
           would have an
           interest in)
       our fathers would make for us
       terrariums,
knife holes peppering Mason jar lids
       the way
in dreams
       we sometimes did each other's hearts.

***

In the yards
       and alleyways at dusk,
           we kids were incandescent with crime.

Fathers and uncles,
       grandfathers and their friends
turned their heads as we performed
       what rites we knew
           to hide the glowing diadems
              of misbehavior.

They were our allies in their fogs of smoke and drink.
        We were both memory and mirror.

***

The boys (and some girls, too), watched
        and learned
        the tricks our fathers used
                to nurse their griefs.

Beer and watered whiskey
                found their way
                into our cups,
                and we joined them
                on the back porch
                while the ball game
                droned on the radio.

Fireflies made of cigarette tips
                glowed in the summer nights.
                We studied our fathers
                in their reverie
                to learn anything we could.
So much of who they were would always elude us.

***

I think of them now
                mostly in summer,
                when I hear the boys in the street
                walking to who knows where
                with their pups and on their skateboards,
                moving toward home in the dark.

And I wonder if I will ever know them,
     those men who loved us,
     hurt us,
         held us,
             made us:

constant accessories
     to our most tender gifts and maladies.

On a Rainy Night, I Look to Li Bai for Advice

A few days
from Christmas. At my desk,
small contentment.

Back in time I go
to visit the old places, alone.

Only one knows me: old Li Bai.
He had his troubles.
I have mine.

The thunder rumbles,
growling out
the ancient truths.

The miles are long.
The years are short.

The ancient poet smiles
and toasts me from his tiny boat.

Magnolia

I wanted for my own
the tender skin
of the magnolia's bloom:
moist, velvet, open.
I saw in them an eye staring
at the heavens in moonlight.
Now and then, in early morning,
they reveal the glint of tears.

Desire was given to me
in my bitterness,
and it nested in the tree of me,
small as a chickadee,
mean as a grackle.

It claimed my heart,
turning it into a hardness
that conceals what I might peel away.

Maybe later,
small seeds of appetite
will poke their way out
like they do the magnolia pod
to remind you of passion.
I'll make of them a necklace,
rosy and sparkling,
littering the earth,
through the swelter
of the dog days of summer.

The little ones know them
for what they are.

Tiny, tempting, secret, sweet.

Heartbreak.

Finials of ache.

Longing.

My Congregations

I sought a congregation of birds,
of shells, of souls, a church
where mourning would be welcome.
I sought a congregation of wildness,
of wilderness, of caverns, a church
where evening could unravel.
I sought a congregation of dreams,
of mothers, of shoes, a church
where woodlands were briared.
I sought a congregation of pines,
of honeysuckle, of cranes,
a church where lives are rattled.
I found a company of letters,
of meadows and snowfalls and foxes.
And there was a gaggle of flowerpots,
of flaws, of fractures, of sparrows,
and a temple of roots, of compost,
of heartbeats, of gargoyles.
That church I found within me,
around me, without me. It speaks
of owls, and bats, and fetters:
all the things I am made of now
that the blight has rescinded.

Part II

THEN

Museum Docent

After Arshile Gorky's The Artist and His Mother

He remembered his mother's
hands as soft,
so he made them look like cotton—
white, yielding, gentle.

It pleased him
that even the littlest children
seeing them together,
mother and son,
remarked on that softness.

He pointed out the whiteness,
the warmth,
the hands like clouds
of dandelion puffs
in August.

And a little hope grew
in his heart to consider
in their lives.

Most of them, he could see,
had received
enough to flutter
their hands
at the memory.

And one or two,
like him,
could only nod
wistfully
at the comparison.

Reading *Owl Moon* to My Niece at Night

After Jane Yolen's Owl Moon

Some evenings, shadows were enough
    to make dark wings on bare brick walls
        like Great Horned's in the story calling
            child and parent into night.

We followed as they trod through snow
    so deep you'd lose a boot in:
        They asked the questions grown-ups did,
            Who *was it* ***who*** *said* ***who?***

You grasped the creases of my sleeve;
        I cupped the bottoms of your feet.
            Owls in the graveyard up the street
              would echo every *who* we made.

Who *are you?* and ***Who*** *knows?*
    Who *cares?* and ***Who*** *loves you?*

A seeker always looks for owls, we said,
    though tracks behind fill steadily with snow.
        She knows it's not too soon for winter's cold.

In the woods, the perched one listens
    from her place high in the pines.
        She crosses the path of the moon
            silently, two wings at a time.

Demeter's Harvest

She was an explorer,
my daughter,
from the minute
she rocked on hands and knees.

Scooting followed,
then tottering,
hard bumps
cushioned
by the earth's
soft nearness.

Loping and running
were the ways
she slipped
into water—oh,
those heart-stopping
steps at each precipice,
the twist a bounce
on the brink
could bring
to my insides!

Fear never
discouraged
mimetic passions.
They were always
her guides.

When he came to us,
I understood them
at last. I was a girl

again, too,
for that dark man
bearing pomegranates.

And then didn't I bring him
my worn-out heart?
And didn't I worship
his rangy looks?
Didn't I caress his brow,
the broken scars of his battles?

And didn't I bathe his back,
scratched and scored
as it was, savoring
his intentions?

Didn't I know
the underworld's king
must want something
when he appears
smiling and pale?

The ground
under our feet
is the underworld's roof,
and every footstep's
an earthquake there;
even the soft trod
of the young girl
as she roams
causes tremors.

Now, the fissures
of shoreline
are rends I send
my sorrows through.
When she is with him,
she is ocean.
When she isn't,
she's all foam,
and winter
is wailing time.

Nothing can reach
into the snowy drifts
I have condemned her to.

Spring is a tentative
thing for us both, but
summer is easier.

We let the bees and locusts
speak for us.

Their drone
is enough.

Family Story

I.

Mother stops folding
laundry for a moment
to look out of the window
at the encroaching twilight.

The white cat walks alone
across the backyard.
It is stalking a bird or bug,
who knows which?

On the swing set,
her daughters sit talking.
They are perched atop it,
surveying their little world.

The rain clouds approach
and the fireflies twinkle.

How sweet the air smells.
How soft everything is
in her hands.

II.

She folds her hands
around the cup of tea
on the table.

Twilight is in her eyes.
It is the fruit
of the haunted hours

she spends writing.
It is not sweet.

III.

Her heart is lodged
in the folds of a fan.
We see it only when her
eyes snap open.
She asks her children
to stop mothering her.
"Take your own risks now.
I've taken my own."

IV.

Her husband,
the king of dusk
gathers up his small followers,
enfolding them in his arms.

He doesn't want them
tagging along
on the heels of his train.

If the king rages,
do his subjects
want his embraces?

Why does the queen
push them toward him,
when his hands are stained
with pain?

A Loss: A Poem in the Voice of My Mother

In memory of Edward Recar

There was a time,
before I lost my French,

I knew enough
to sing with tunes
my grandpa crooned.

I remember being four
and spoiled with all his sugar sweets

as he toted me
upon his back
around the gallery.

***

We'd end up in the kitchen
at the pantry shelves

where I would root around
to my small heart's content.

I liked the pictures of the kids
on cookie tins and apple cans.

He said one day I'd have my own;
I'd shake my head
as he would laugh
and then the two of us
would put them back again.

***

One year I got the influenza bad.
He wrapped me up
and drove us
down the lanes.

My mom had lost
three boys before,
Roy and Floyd
and David,
who I never knew.

***

It seems all wrong
he doesn't have a stone,

nor iron cross
to mark the place he lays.

One year, my daddy paced it off
for me, from an old dogwood tree,

but now that tree is gone.
All I know
is he's in Richwoods' churchyard there.
He died in summer.
I do remember that.

****

My uncles made the coffin
they put him in.
Poor folks laid them out at home still
in those days.

I wasn't scared,
until I understood
and watched
my mother covering
our few mirrors one by one,
saying we don't want
his soul caught here at home.

****

When she found me
on a chair,
pulling all the pillowcases off,
she spanked me hard
and sent me out
into the yard.

I sat out on the porch
and cried and cried all day,
knowing he never would have minded
that I'd wanted him to stay.

Icarus

The only fire Icarus could see
as he glided across the fields
of Sardinia

was the sun
and its gloating reflection
on the sea.

The stars that he knew
were hidden. Planets
his father had named
were unknown to him.

Once airborne,
he took the lead,
as young men are inclined to.
He had found to his delight
a few pumps of his arms
would hoist him midair.

If the breeze had stayed cool
and if the sun's rays
had not been warm
or if the ether had not tempted him
in its entirety
giddiness would never have overcome him.

But did Icarus feel
the fear we are tempted
to ascribe to him?

Hadn't he done the impossible?
The thing that men
were never meant to do?

What would there have been
afterward?
Unbelievable stories
to tell the grandchildren
year after year?

With a few quick beats
of the arms, he was gone.
And the father
followed, anxious
and resigned.

Then suddenly,
the beauty
of the fall,
a youth tumbling
over and over
again
into the sea.

The quiet was disturbed
by a few birds,
waves, and an old man's wail.

For a moment,
a small cloud
of feathers
everywhere.

Regarding Dr. Gachet

> *"I have a portrait of Dr. Gachet with the heartbroken*
> *expression of our time."*
>
> > —*From a letter from Vincent to Theo van Gogh*

His head is eclipsed by the moon
of his white cap. The bells
of the flowers beside him
ring peals of cleaving.

Should the fissures of heart
be pried wide? What god
to appease: mind or art?

My lover, who wears no
white cap, hides his lacunae,
though rents and tears are just
visible beneath his frayed sleeves.

If you would reach toward his brow,
he'd pull back, rejecting the small gesture
as too sentimental for him, like
the foxgloves on the table
and the doctor's golden hair.

The expression of Dr. Gachet's heart
can be no different from ours:
it's one of hubris or pathos or joy
in a gravity of longing.

Renunciation

After St. Francis Renounces Worldly Goods *by*
Giotto, San Francesco in Assisi Basilica, 1295

What could we say
after that—when you
walked into town
naked as Adam?

The bishop,
chagrined at the sight,
handed over his cope
so you would be swathed.

How could you think
we would not feel fury,
when you'd been given
the very best that we had?

That Great Hand
from the sky
you say blesses
your endeavors—
no one but you
sees such sights
anymore.

The robes,
and tasseled cap,
didn't matter;
the medallion
was a memento,
of your mother—

what use
can they be
to nightjars
perched
along the walls?

Beautiful boy,
your congregation
soars high
above you,
paying no mind
to your poems.

Oh, my son,
you will
never know
its love
the way you might
have known ours—
not while you cast
your heart
like barley
on the hard
and wintery loam.

On Lazarus

I never wanted him risen,
the man who used fists
with his anger.

I never mourned at his passing.
I thrilled to the shroud.

I rejoiced in the sight
of his organ, flaccid
in death
as we washed him.

That pleasure could never
be bested by any gift
thrust into my hands.

But then he was raised
from the grave,
to be guided
by others forever.

And then, little sister,
I wanted him
alive in your hands,

to dwell a while at your justice,
your whims, your griefs—
at your mercy,

and learn the pain
of your silence,
your dignity
through all of his crimes.

When I Was Twenty-Four

> *Based on a passage from* The Journal
> of Eugène Delacroix.

It was twilight, and the town clock
in the square of Ablution
had just struck nine or ten.
I sat in the dusk,
on the path to the lake.

You had dined with us,
and after my mother
went to bed, we strolled it,
noting the birds
heading home to roost.
That night my sister
sat reading the paper,
as I studied a book
about Caravaggio.

In the somber sky,
a big orange moon
climbed slowly
between the trees.
My sister talked
with her friends
about love,
and my brother Tom
crooned some lyrics
I used to know.
His voice
wasn't pleasant
in the usual sense,

but his baritone
was musical.

He wore his heart
on his sleeve
when he sang;
I remembered
when he was just
a boy and worried
about everything.
He was so fragile then.

And now, I suppose,
I must leave
them both
and the home
that I love.
Everyone grows up,
that's what
I told myself.
I laughed
that there were
ever days
when I tried to stop.

They haunt me
like a charming memory,
a flower
by the wayside.

Keys

These three were in the house
when we first moved in. The other two,
the small brass one

and the one in the red guard
saying "front door,"
don't belong here;
They were to Clematis,
and I forgot about them
when we finally sold the place.

But the one with the hexagon
head is the one from Antoinette Street.
I gave it to you that spring when we became lovers.

Ten years now we've
been gone from that place
where you would come in late.

I'd pretend I was asleep
when all along, I'd been waiting up
for you.

Imagine me on the balcony
a forty-year-old Juliet.
Or think of me swimming
long after the pool had closed.

I risked a lot when I risked
my heart. Is it wrong
to wish us back there sometimes?

Open your hand,
and then grasp the key
I push into your palm so fiercely.

It's for those days
you want to enter again
those sweet, locked rooms.

The Lovers

After Utamaro

Four thin fingers clasping
the moon of her shoulder.
        Her loosened obi.
        Her neck a calyx, an egret's.
        Her kimono anikki falling open.

Mushroom grows in opacate cellar.
        His rumpled hakama.
        His oiled queue.
        His pale feet bare of tabi.

Arms embrace hips the way
snow girds carnelian stones.

        The katana and the halberd.
        The monument and the sheaf.
        The shrine and the scripture.
        The tatami. The moon.
        His snail. Her shell.

**Tu Fu Dreams of Fishing
with his Wife at Wu Gorge**

Her pole lax beside his,
a basket of fish sits
at her feet, waiting
to be scaled.

                 Carp
have been biting well.
It's damp and misty,
but there's a flask
of good plum wine
and in the knapsack,
dumplings for two.

            Despite
the cold and wet,
the old girl wears
a little bit of rouge.

It's nice to have her nearby
in travel,
even if she's a dream
who talks too much.

Her chatter is sonorous
to even the silver gill
darting about
like her fishy retinue.

In the gloom,
her catch,
like her smile,

is luminescent
and flittering.

****

He can't speak a word
of loss. That old goat Li Po
will tease him unmercifully.

So,
in the poem he will write
when he wakes,
it's Li Po he will toast to.

****

Old Li Po!

It's a rueful thing
to be homesick,
drunk and howling
at the rabbit moon!

How seldom
and how slowly
the practices of art
soothe and delectate
the poor and desolate
human heart.

Wicker Weaving in New Guinea

I've cut my hands so many times while weaving
I like the paste
they're patched with
of reeds and blood and clay.

When I wove in New Guinea,
I would head out early
to gather rushes
and buckets of clay.

I would forget the reasons
to leave dawn alone,
out in the places
where the Aborigines go.

I sought all the places
the brown houseboys
would sneak their cigars.
I watched as they wrestled
each other down. Watched
as they planted their heels
and raised their brows,
interrupted
in some childhood game.

I couldn't leave it out there
under the stones. Would I find
baskets or yellowed bones?

I still like working at dawn,
alone. I wish I could tell you
about those bones. But all
real stories are told in the
weaving. In the twisted reeds.
In the rust-colored handles.

Francis and the Birds

He fed them all: the crotchety geese,
the pushy hens, partridges
with their topknots.
Waddling plovers gorged on
gestating grain
and swallows and sparrows
stopped squabbling
over breadcrumbs.

They listed to him
for it seemed unkind not to.
Of his preaching,
they understood not one word.
He seemed not to mind,
since they were like most folk,
though they did not avoid him
when he came around.

His consolations reminded the birds
of their own songs,
the assent of his coos,
chiding clucks, and *trrwhits*.
His caws needed practice,
and his cheeps were too high,
but at least they admitted
he avoided those honks.

Patiently they brought him along,
attending thoughtfully,
and replying softly in kind.

For the air around him was gold,
and this was the way
they knew him for one of their own.
It shimmered as it did
as they dipped and looped,
glided and swooped
and even waddled
on warm afternoons.

They masked their disappointments
on the hours he wasted on men,
who didn't understand a word
of the language of motion,
something even the trees
had a handle on, deaf
as they were to the birds.

See here, in this image,
how the cypress leans toward him,
eager to offer him some gentle advice?
What do you think it would be,
to that small, dark man, wandering
the hills cradling sparrows in his palms?

Faith

That faith
you don't have:
water
never made
into wine—

your bread stretches
out on it,
sodden and limp.
Not even the geese
seem to want it.

What ark can be
supplied with
such offerings,
you wonder.
What temple
you've built
can house
the meager god
you cannot see?

Turned stones
reveal beetles
and dank earth.
What's within
that can woo
briars
into blooms?

It's not just fear
making stray forays
through the rooms
in which you sleep.
The heart is there:
the cynosure
of wisdom.

And about that bread:
of course, the geese
will eventually find it
and devour it greedily
even as you walk away.

They cannot name
the hand that makes
such bounties appear.

They're just there
on the water
you won't dip
a toe into,
right at the moment
they could use
a boon.

Magnolia Memoria

After Hurricane Laura

The magnolia was once a reality.
The earth was littered with leaves,
and a few white bowls stood waiting
on the branches of the tree.

They were as open as bows on ladies' hats.
Silver as my mother's hair. Soon, I think,
they'll match my own,
and then, like hers, begin to drift away.

But last night, the storm.

So today, the magnolia is an old dream. The earth
is bathed in sunlight. No more white bowls.
Blue jays circle the yard, looking for landing places.
The last petals are brown as the sugar
atop a crème brûlée,
or the color of my niece's skin.

I stand beneath a sky where the magnolia, now,
is just an idea. A sky where love is an idea, like justice.
Coins for a parking meter
rattle in my pocket. The lone cloud
up there is the color of a robin's egg
in the center of a morning glory.

I stand in the street
puzzling over the heat
thinking I was never a lover
of the magnolia's

profligate pods.
Their red
tongues bursting out,
mocking my displeasure.

But for its leaves, its scent, its generous blooms
I grieve like a mother
of a daughter.
I knew its faults and gifts
intimately
and loved its promises
every year,
oh, so deeply.

Part III

WHEN?

The Word for When

> *After* The Meaning of Tingo
> *by Adam Jacot de Boinod*

A single word in Inuit
describes the way
I pace my porch,
hoping you'll be back
for a tryst:

      iktsuarpok

And there's a word
on Easter Island
for that man
who takes
your things

one
         by
                one

till you are left
with nothing at all.
That word is

      tingo

I'm afraid
I've learned
a word explaining
all the ways
I make

what's bad
much worse,
a little Indonesian word:

        neko-neko

In deepest Congo
there's a word
for one who
pardons twice
but then no more.
That word's

        ilunga

but my favorite
word's in Danish.
It names those gates
that open only once then

        close forever.

It evokes panic
as all your chances
are used up.

        Torschlusspanik

****

What are some words,
you ask, for cooling love,
or for loving for the last time?

aki ga tatsu (in Japanese)

and

onsia (among the Boro)

The saddest word
I know
is an old Turkish one,
reminding us
not every house
is where the heart is

        berhane

And when I hear it,
I can't help but think
of my poor heart,
a rambling place,
which is what *berhane* means,
a mansion impractically large,

                a place too large
                        for one soul
                                to keep up.

The Way to Read a Triptych

The weeping boughs spring back
from right to left after snows.
The winesaps you know
will not stay barren; you'll see,
they'll soon be burgeoning.

The barn door will not list
on its solitary hinge,
not if you read the heart
the way the ancients did.

In Tu Fu's orchard, trees
are always in full in flower.
Fences glare with new rails,
sharp and white.

Memory is that road that leads
from winter to spring:
forget those lands where books
are read another way.

In our east, triptychs lead
from decay to bloom.

This is the order of things
in the garden, after all,
and not a petition
for how things ought to be.

My Mother's Communion

One day soon, I think, my mother
will rise, don her faith like a knight
his armor, and proceed down the aisle
to God's side, presenting arms to the lock-
jawed priest who knows
her sin, who dares
to keep from her what she
has come to claim from him.
Nose to nose, priest and sinner
pose on this earthly brink.

He will weigh the costs of refusing,
glare into her steely eyes,
look behind her at the throng
of others who are sinners, too,
then finally find the compassion
a man of God should have,
and give her bread and move on
down the line. Returning to her seat,
she'll smile (at least I hope so)—not because
she's done the penance he required
so long ago, but because she
has finally decided to show him
she will not live a lifetime of it.

The Selkie's Children

They were always more his
than mine,
with their light hair and blue eyes.

Those wholly mine waited
in the waters. From the shore,
I'd see them watching,
their soft brown eyes glistening.

One evening I was feeding
Davey, when my eldest sea-born
made his way up to the house.

In his puppy language,
he begged me come home. I cannot tell you
how it made my heart break
to wave him off.

I've looked in every place,
for my coat that had been taken.

And I can hear the barks and moans
of my folk coming up from the beach.

What I am, they are,
though the man disagrees
and hides it,
as he hides my skin from me.

Someday, he who robbed me
of my skin and my self
will know the loneliness
and yearning
I've known these seven years.

In my dreams, I see all my children
playing games together in the waves.

My selkie brood swims
with their land-born kin.
And none of us—no, none of us—with secrets then.

The Emperor's Dreams

I. The Child Emperor of the Moon

I was a child who looked at the moon
and thought there were people living there.
They were tiny as butterflies,
and they sparkled in the dark.

I was no emperor then, though I knew
someday, I would be one there,
for on Earth I was an emissary, a sage,
a budding artist.

Moonlight always robes the emperor
in neomenium; fireflies are jewels
in his crown.

I was a child that loved crowns; people
often called me Selene.

Skirting pools of moonlight
and diving into its basins,
Callisto called me and guided the way.

II. The Emperor of the Moon

The Emperor of the Moon
would rather regard fireflies
than contemplate the scrolls on his desk.

Reports, assignments, taxes, and troops,
he cannot sweep them away as he wants to.

He was once a child who studied satellites
through his uncle's telescope. He gazed at seas,
distant shores, and bottomless craters.

In his dreams, he was an emissary visiting
remote lands named Amalthea, Europa, Callisto.

He longed to dine with friend and foe alike
at its apogee. But those days are over.
If he retires, he will write his book,
or become a monk who studies the stars.

Perhaps one day, he'll dream
once more of being an emperor,
the child emperor of the moon.

Rumi and Francis

Rumi would have understood
why Francis
threw off his garments.

They were hot. They itched.
They pulled.
They weighed heavy
on his skin.

Rumi would have invited him
to the hammam, where they
would have lolled
in the water,
Francis explaining
how the steam
in the sunlight reflected
God's breath
and how their puckered skin
could be celebrated
as God's kiss.

Rumi would have lingered,
discussing ecstasy,
a thing to be experienced,
"for words, my friend,
cannot describe it,
though I try
as I dance."

Ecstasy did not frighten
Francis, a man
who had conversed
with wolves and bears
on the philosophy
of love.

In the dawn light,
Rumi would see
what the boy's
own father could not—
a young man ready
to bare everything:
his heart, his body,

his soul,
and most of all,
his nascent/absent fears.

Vincent in the Garden of the Asylum at Saint-Rémy

The yellow house at the end of the track
peeks out of the trees, beckoning more
than the camellias that stand in the foreground.

The little bench in the shade of the maple tree
has no occupant, an invitation
written in oil to the lonely.

Blues and greys are a solace, the garden
a crèche of greens and yellows, a palette
of quietude for the hand that danced and darted
until sparrows alit on the bench.

Then they both paused: hand and bird,
studying each other
until the light faded and the camellias
dropped their blooms.

They do not perch there, now, those little birds.
They have flown away, leaving the bench empty.

The one who never rested there moved on
to paint other rooms, other birds, other gardens.
We have seen his flocks in other skies,
this quiet garden abandoned and darkening.

The Third Wish of the Pirate's Wife

My third wish would be
of all you gambled away,
the wind, the watch,
and the twenty-two dollars
you were going to spend on Jameson's,
the hook you gave up be found.
You'd bet the most precious thing you had.

I grieve the loss of that hook keenly.
I loved its iciness.

Ach, the chills
it gave me as it traveled down my spine
or between my thighs
you moving it so gently.

Yes, it frightened me sometimes
but not as much as you frighten me now:

hookless,
handless,
maybe heartless,
without cash, liquor, or honey
within reach.

An Idea of North

For Minik Wallace (1890–1918) and his father,
Qisuk, tragically brought to New York by Robert Peary

He had an idea about it. About its whiteness.
        About its coldness.
                Its stillness and whiteness.

It began with a woman's voice
             and ended with a man's.

No children spoke in it.
        No young boys.
               No stick-legged girls.

He had an idea of north
             and it began with a voice
                    talking about it.

About its light.
        About Qisuk.
               Then Qisuk speaking of it.

A man walks on the ice.
        His boots crunkle it.

Those grumbling soles.
        The chill beneath them.

Qisuk now floats
        on an armature of wire
               in the museum of north.

But not true north.
> A white man's north.
>> A preserve of cold.
>>> An athenaeum of death.

Where men in it are cold as meteorites.

This son speaks of north and of fathers.
> Speaks to friends.
>> Not good friends. Not strangers.

Not anyone who understands his pain.

If he can find a way, he'll learn about north.
> Know it as Qisuk did.
>> As Greenland does.
>>> As ice and dogs know it.

And when Minik brings Qisuk home,
> Qisuk's bones, that is.
> No longer relics. No longer exhibits.

> Minik will then see
>> if his memory of north
>> is what north is.

>> What he hopes it is.

A place where a man's bones
          and his soul
                    can rest together

                         beneath
                              the sky
                         beneath
                              a counterpane of snow.

A Bone Poem

They're uncovering them all the time,
ours never as white as mastodons',
lawyers' seldom picked clean,
soldiers' patched over and over,
and the little ones always so sad.

Few can relinquish
all feeling
when entering
the field of bones.

But eventually, we'll all shine,
all bones brought into light.

Some will admire the knobby ends;
some note the nice, clean breaks.
Others will mourn the hardened centers,
the missing partners
dust beneath their feet.

Most of all they'll wonder
what we were and were not
at our last meeting.

Oh, for those days again
when we had everything,
and you could tell one
from the other.

In Pissarro's *Spring, Plum Blossoms*

In Pissarro's *Spring,*
Plum Blossoms,
Pontoise, the tree's blooms
hide the blue roofs
and whitewashed walls
of the town's modest houses.

And while the inn
on the hill
is sometimes
full of tourists,
mostly
it's occupied
by the owner's in-laws.

Birds sing faintly
above it all,
the streets
and the parks around it
are never deserted.

There was a time,
when roses
appeared in the cheeks
of weathered old men.
A time when peaches
turned succulent
in the hands of greying wives.

We loved in such a time,
a spring when sparrows
were raucous
with all they could profess.

It is raining just a little,
the sky grey
with puffy clouds.

A patch of azure creeps into
the painting, promising
clear days ahead.

A hydrangea blooms
next to a little dog
resting a moment
before he sets out to wander
the wet streets unleashed.

Is the spring
in this painting
enough
to draw us close,
even if you
and I are not really
beneath
the plum blossoms
of Pontoise?

Shall we love again,
as we did before,
mon chéri?
Shall we give
the little nonexistent sparrows
something outré to profess?

The New Gardener's Questions

A small brown frog lives beneath
    the white azalea shrub
        behind the yellow daffodils
            I planted
                with my mother.

New gardener that I am,
    I know a little about buds,
        something about blooms,
            and even less
                about frogs.

Will he kill my yellow day lilies
    with his little cave of mud?
        Will a plague of his little sisters
            descend like a horde
                upon my yard?

Should I make my place
    as uninhabitable to him
        as I have tried to
            to the cats
                who shit in my mulch?

Why do the ants
    still live in my walls,
        and the wasps still
            nest in my bricks?

Why do weird worms consume
    the leaves of my cannas
        and banana spiders spin curtains
            across my porch?

These are all deep questions,
      as deep as those
            I ask at night in bed:
                 How will I live if he leaves?
                    When will I forget him?
                       And who, little frog, will I love?